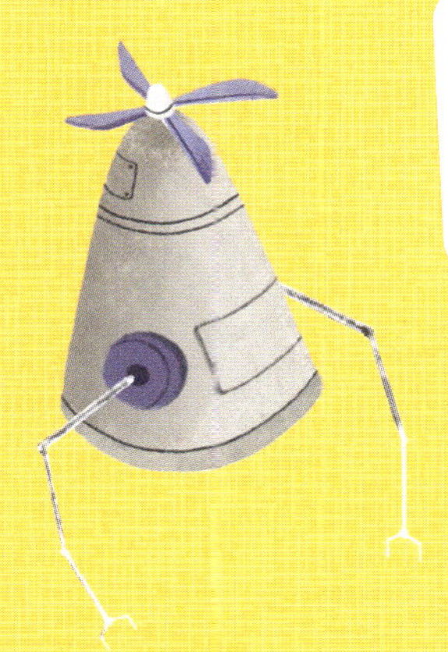

I0820437

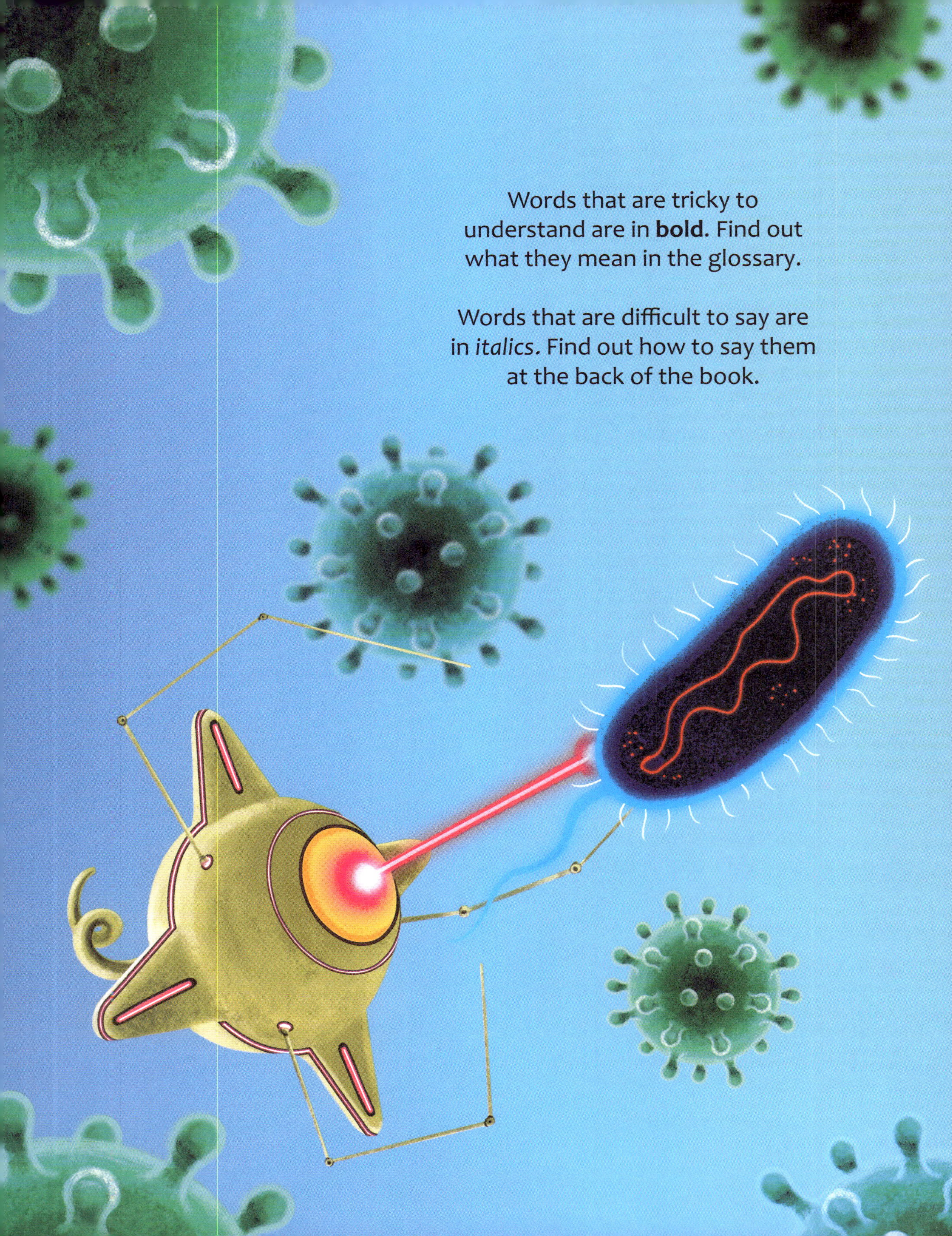

Words that are tricky to understand are in **bold**. Find out what they mean in the glossary.

Words that are difficult to say are in *italics*. Find out how to say them at the back of the book.

# CAN THESE TINY ROBOTS CHANGE OUR WORLD?

*DISCOVER THE SCIENCE BEHIND* ***NANOTECHNOLOGY***
*(nah-noh-TECK-noh-luh-jee)*

*Written by Olivia Watson*
*Illustrated by Daniel Limon*

## WHAT IS NANOTECHNOLOGY?

*Nanotechnology* is a branch of science and engineering that designs and builds things on the **nanoscale,** using **atoms** to make things work in new and special ways.

The scientists who study nanotechnology are called **NANOTECHNOLOGISTS.**

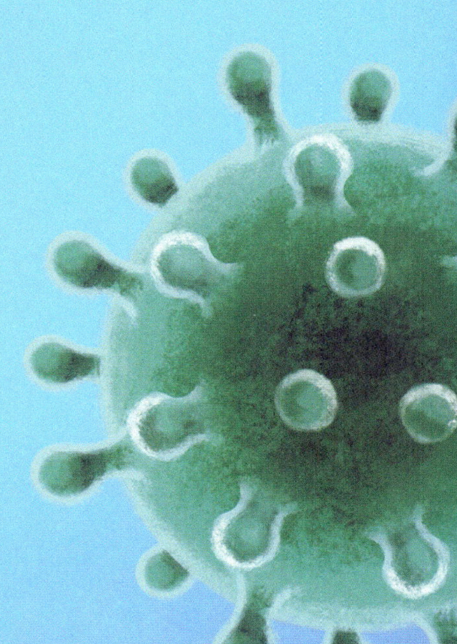

"What will the world be like in the future?" is one of humanity's biggest questions. When we think of the future, we may picture human-like **robots**, high-tech cities, and flying cars.

We may think of solving problems like illnesses and **climate change.** Some scientists say that to think big, you have to first think small – very small...

*Nanotechnologists* are talented scientists and engineers who study and build things that are so small they can only be seen with incredibly strong microscopes. Because of this, they have their own system for measuring – they use nanometers/nanometres (nm)!

The difference between one nm and one regular meter/metre is even bigger than the difference between the size of **a golf ball and the Earth!**

Nanotechnologists are creating special robots called **nanobots.** These machines are so small they can be put into living things' bodies to help in ways normal machines can't!

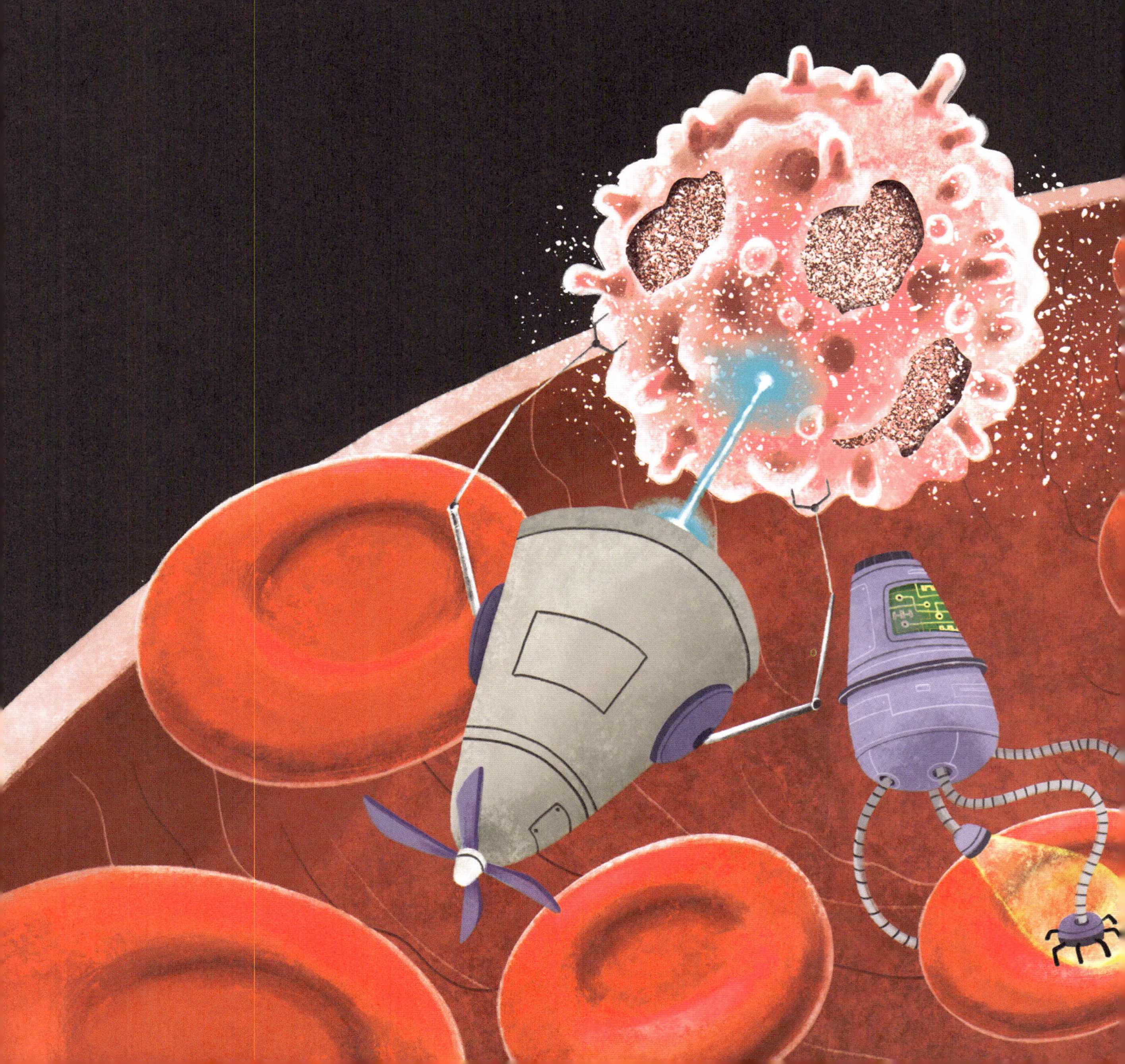

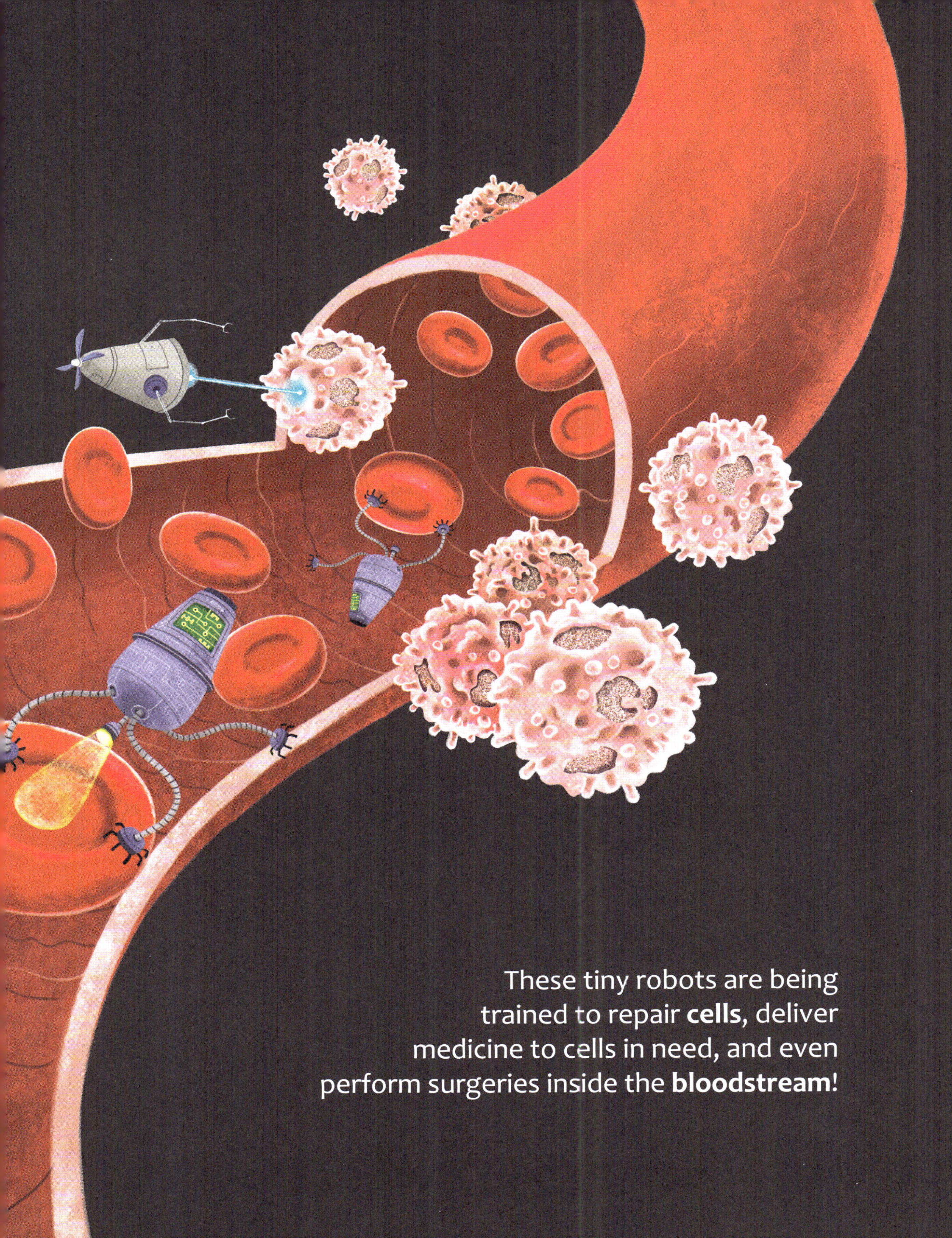

These tiny robots are being trained to repair **cells**, deliver medicine to cells in need, and even perform surgeries inside the **bloodstream**!

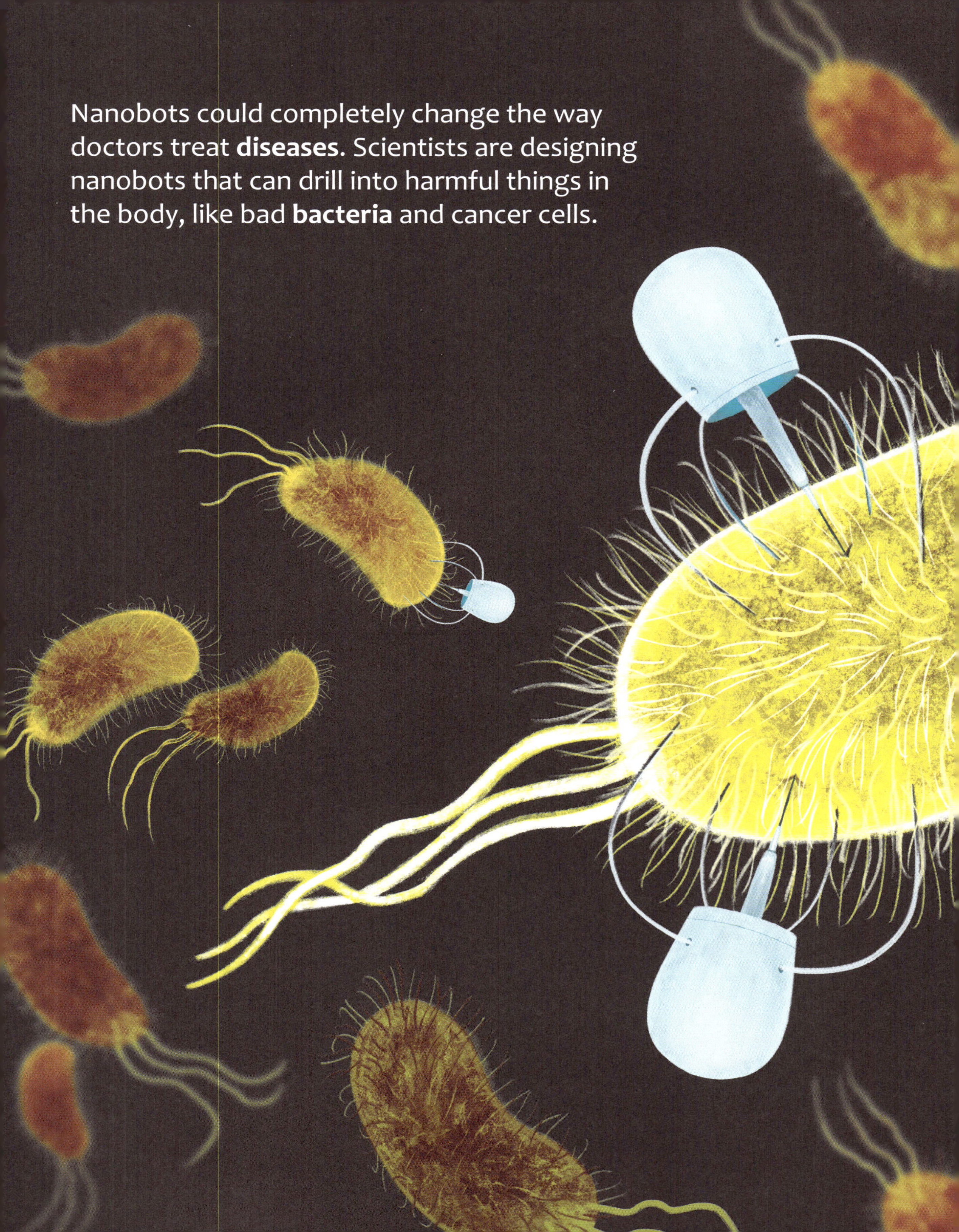

Nanobots could completely change the way doctors treat **diseases.** Scientists are designing nanobots that can drill into harmful things in the body, like bad **bacteria** and cancer cells.

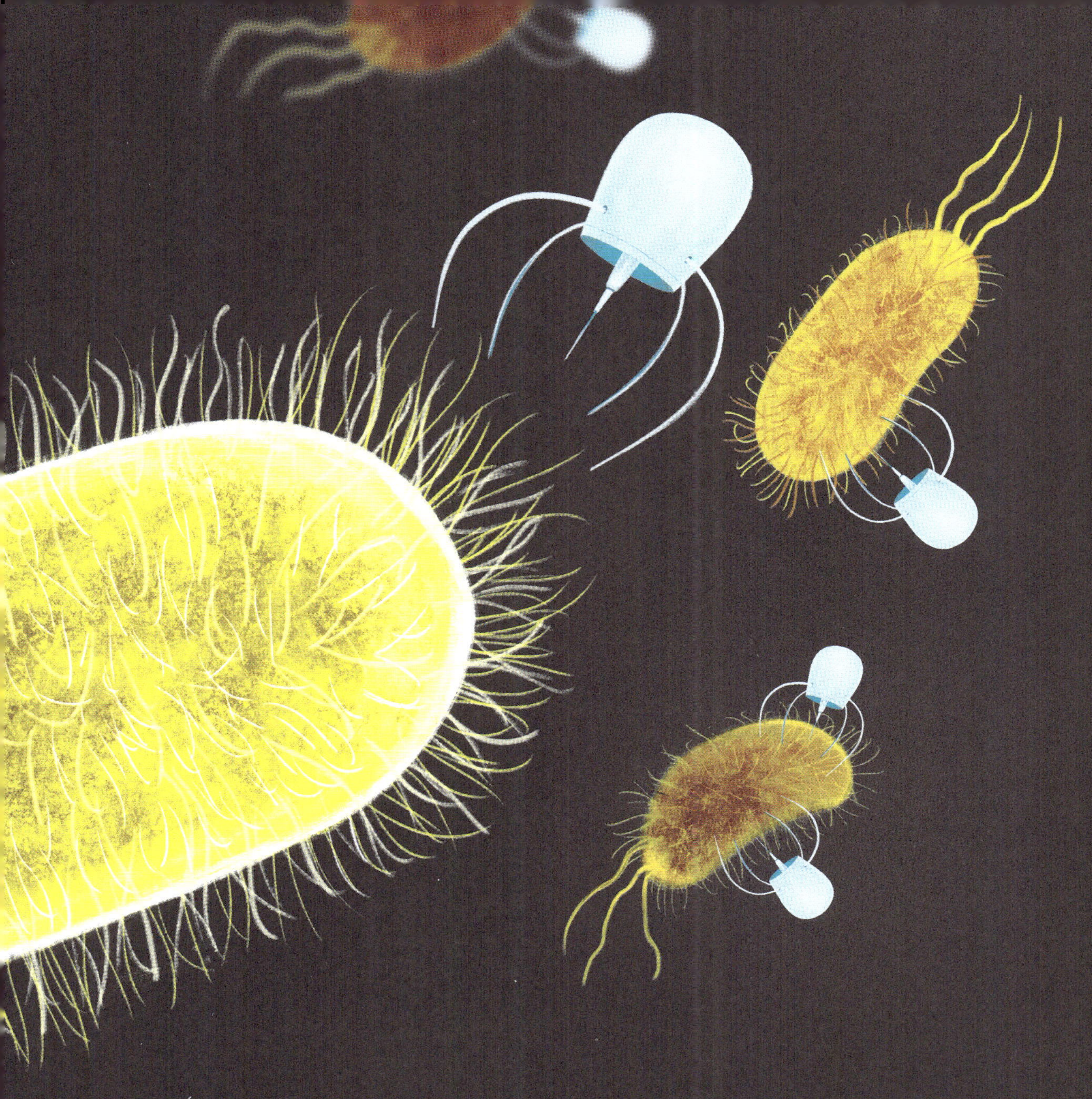

By destroying these dangerous **organisms** and cells from the inside out, nanobots could help people fight off illnesses and recover quicker. These tiny robots could be **real life-savers!**

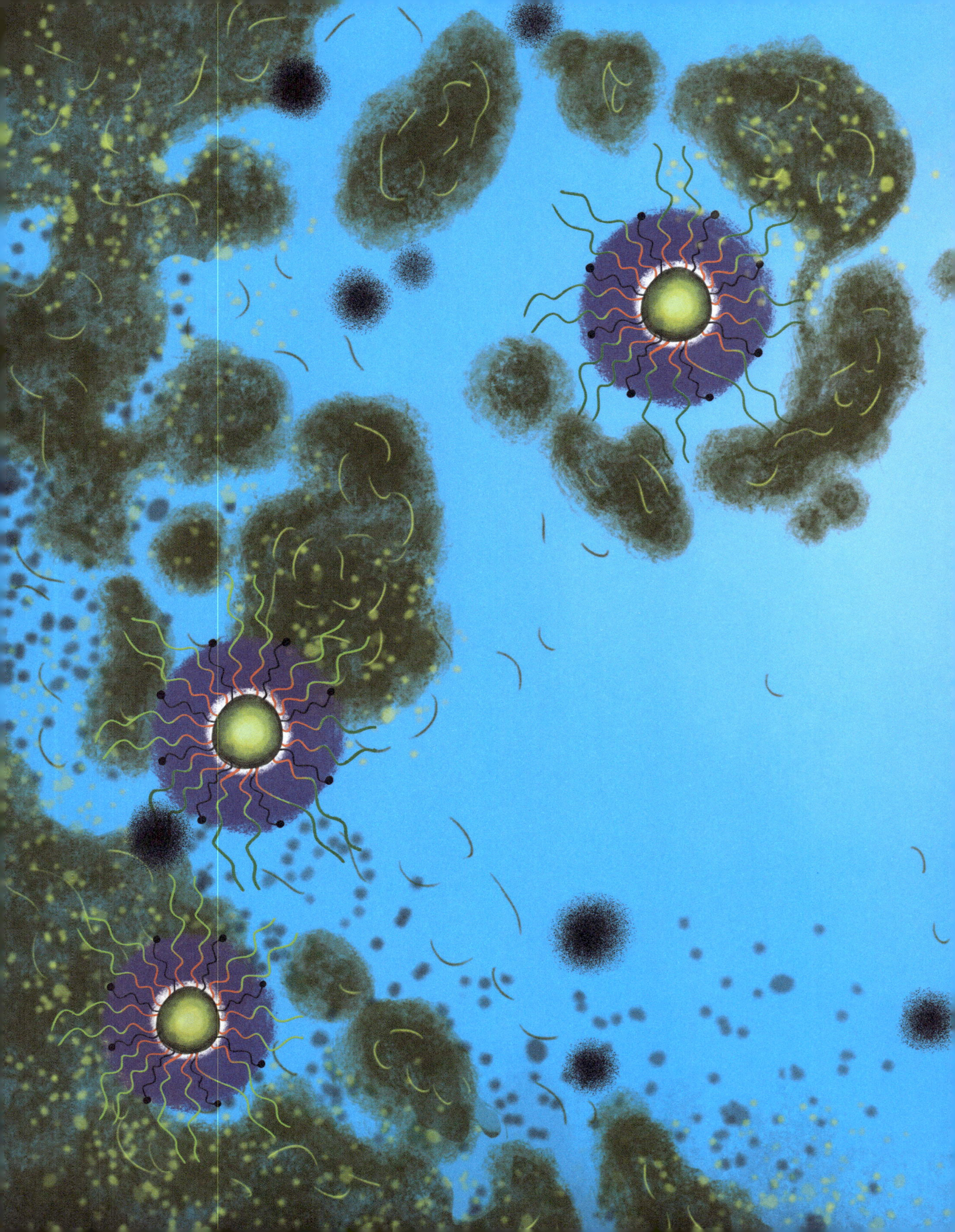

Nanobots won't just be sent into the human body, they can be used in nature too!

Nanotechnology could help strip bacteria and **pollution** out of dirty water. This would make water cleaner and safer for people and animals to drink.

Fixing problems on Earth would be great, but this technology won't stop there. It could help repair the **ozone layer,** high up in Earth's **atmosphere.** This layer, which shields Earth from the Sun's harmful **UV rays,** has become damaged. Repairing it would protect all life on Earth from these strong rays.

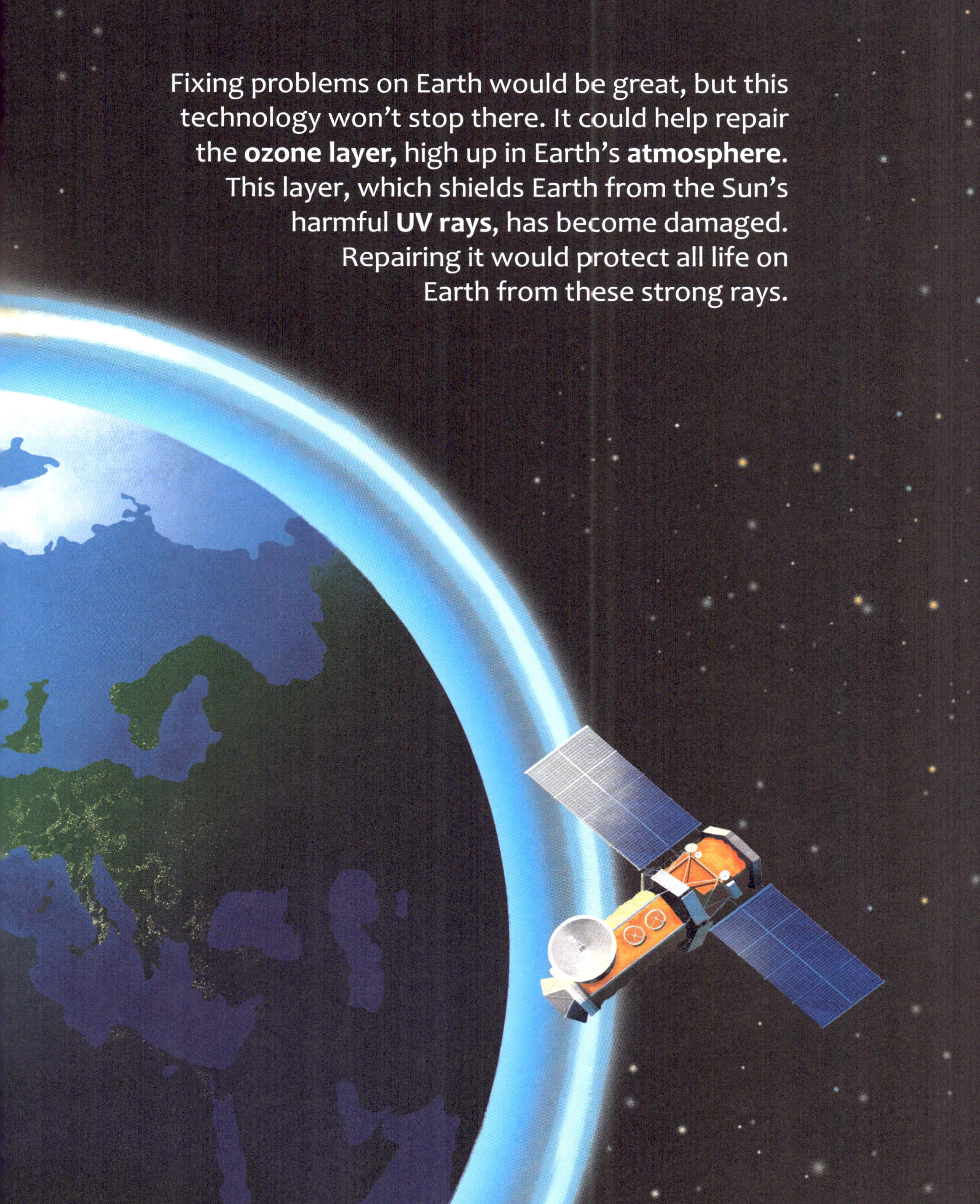

With nanotechnology, the sky's no longer the limit! Nanobots could repair damage to spacecraft and satellites while in outer space, meaning missions could last longer! But nanobots aren't the only thing nanotechnologists study...

They've found that **modifying** materials on the nanoscale changes what they can do. This could make spacecraft lighter and stronger, helping them travel further.

To survive these missions, nanomaterials must cope with harsh conditions, like extreme temperatures and high levels of **radiation**. Scientists hope to test their inventions on Venus, a hot, unforgiving planet that has **acid rain**.

This technology won't just help scientists learn about outer space, but how to successfully send machines to dangerous places on Earth where humans can't go.

That's not the only way nanotechnology is helping us do things we've never done before. Thanks to this amazing science, engineers can create complicated nanoscale electronics. They've already made cameras the size of a grain of salt and drones smaller than a speck of dust.

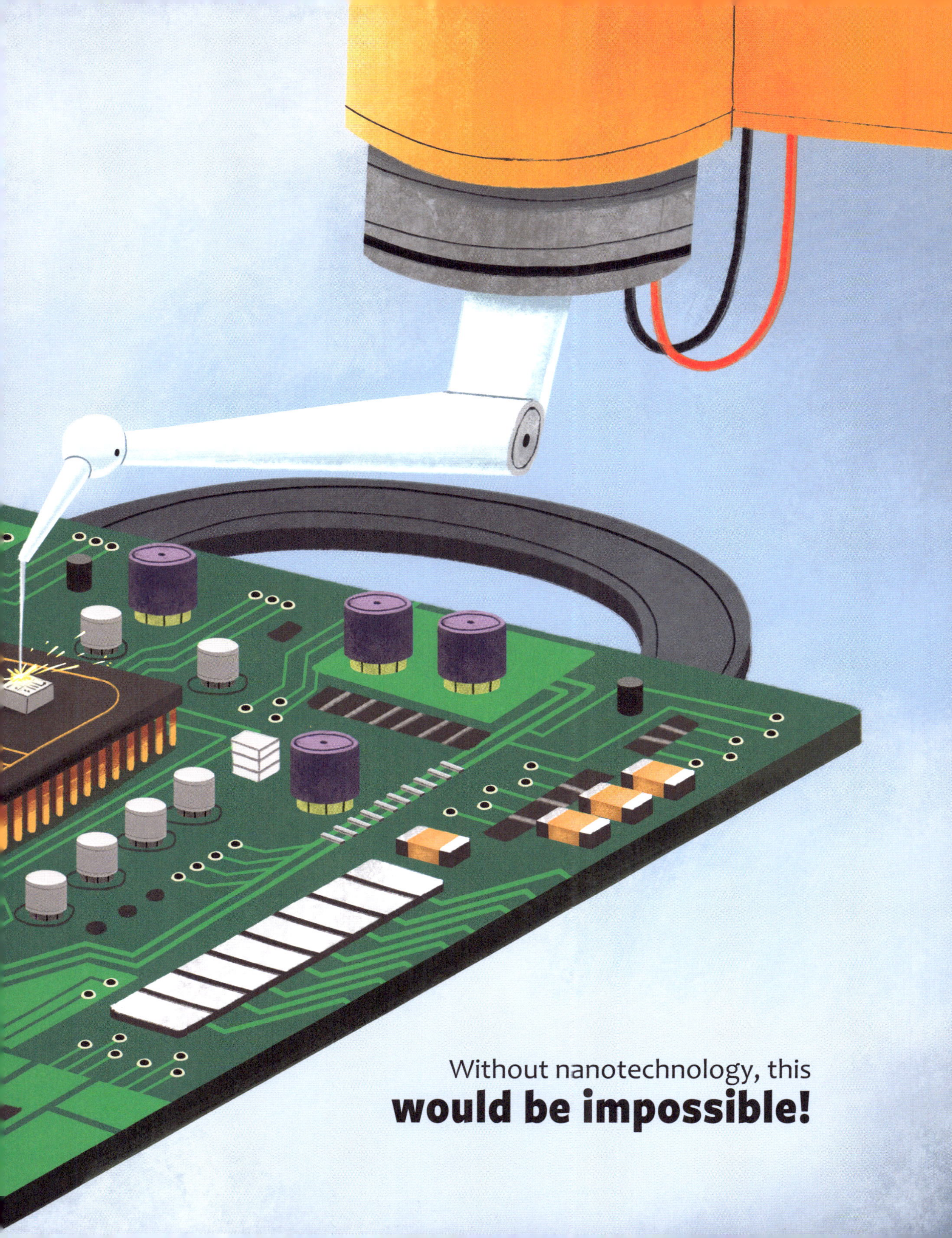

Without nanotechnology, this
**would be impossible!**

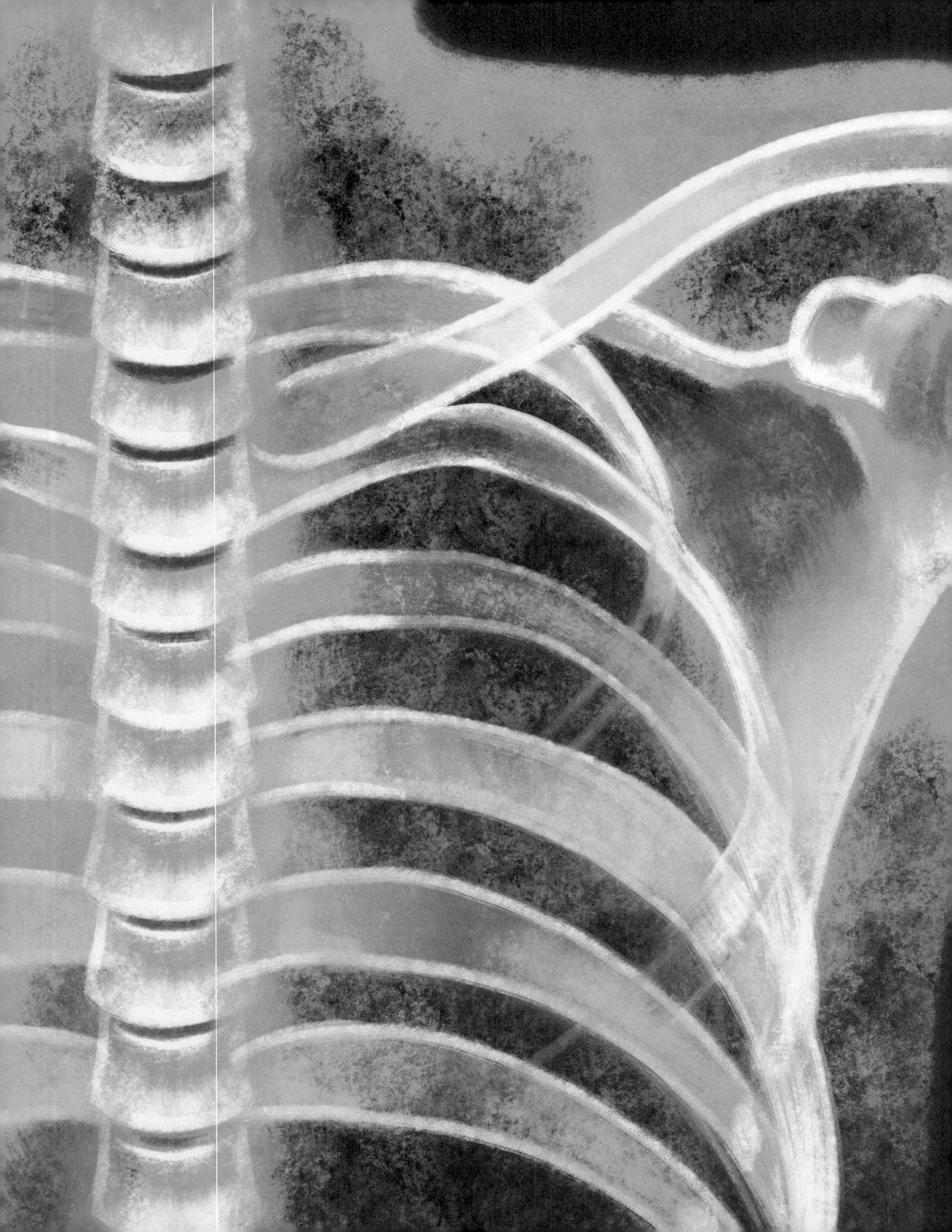

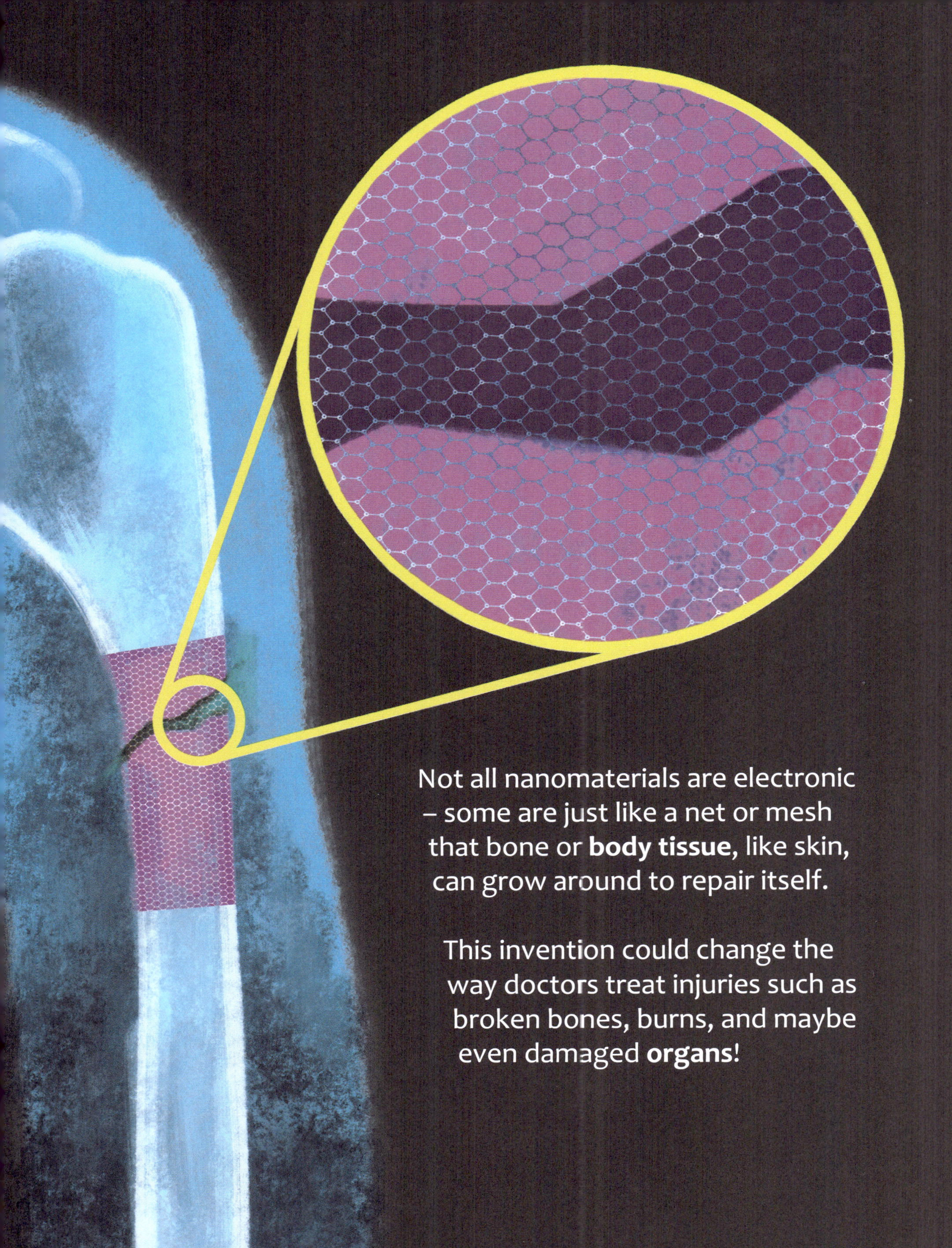

Not all nanomaterials are electronic – some are just like a net or mesh that bone or **body tissue**, like skin, can grow around to repair itself.

This invention could change the way doctors treat injuries such as broken bones, burns, and maybe even damaged **organs**!

If nanotechnology helps us live longer, we will need more food! **Nanoparticles** can carry important **nutrients** that help plants grow. It's easier for plants to **absorb** tiny particles, meaning farmers can grow more food with fewer **chemicals**, keeping farmland healthier.

In real life, nanoparticles are too small for magnifying glasses like this one to see!

That's not the only way nanomaterials can help us look after our planet. They can catch and remove harmful **gases** from the air and replace plastic in items like batteries and computer screens. They can even make solar panels more effective at collecting the Sun's power and turning it into **clean energy**!

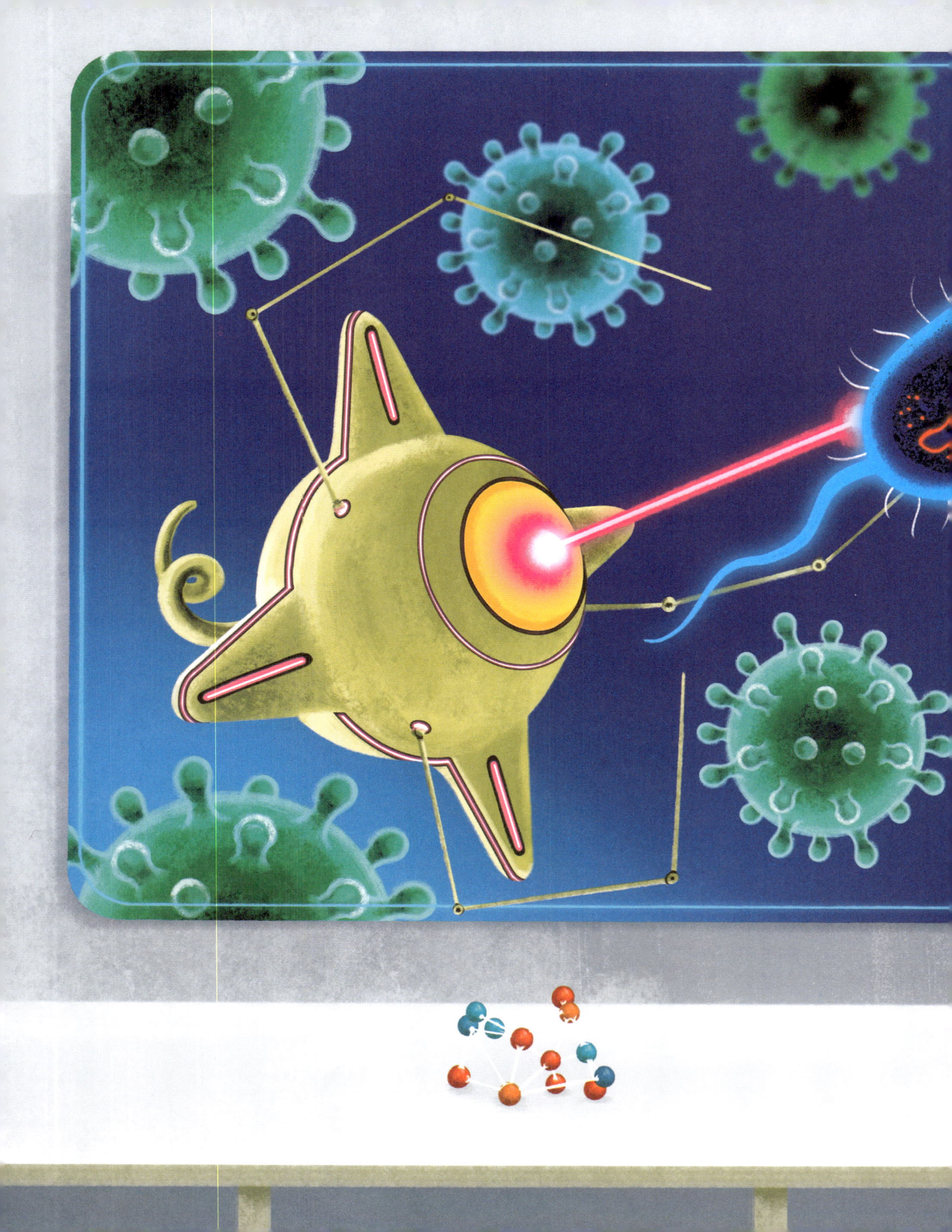

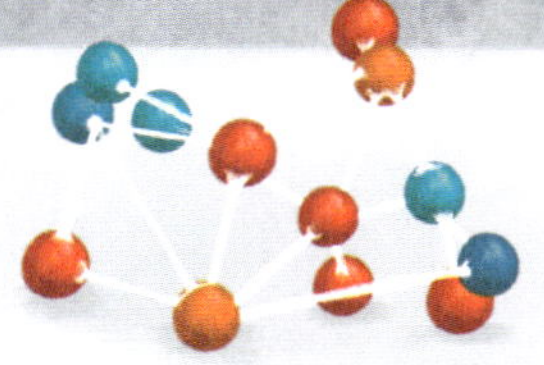

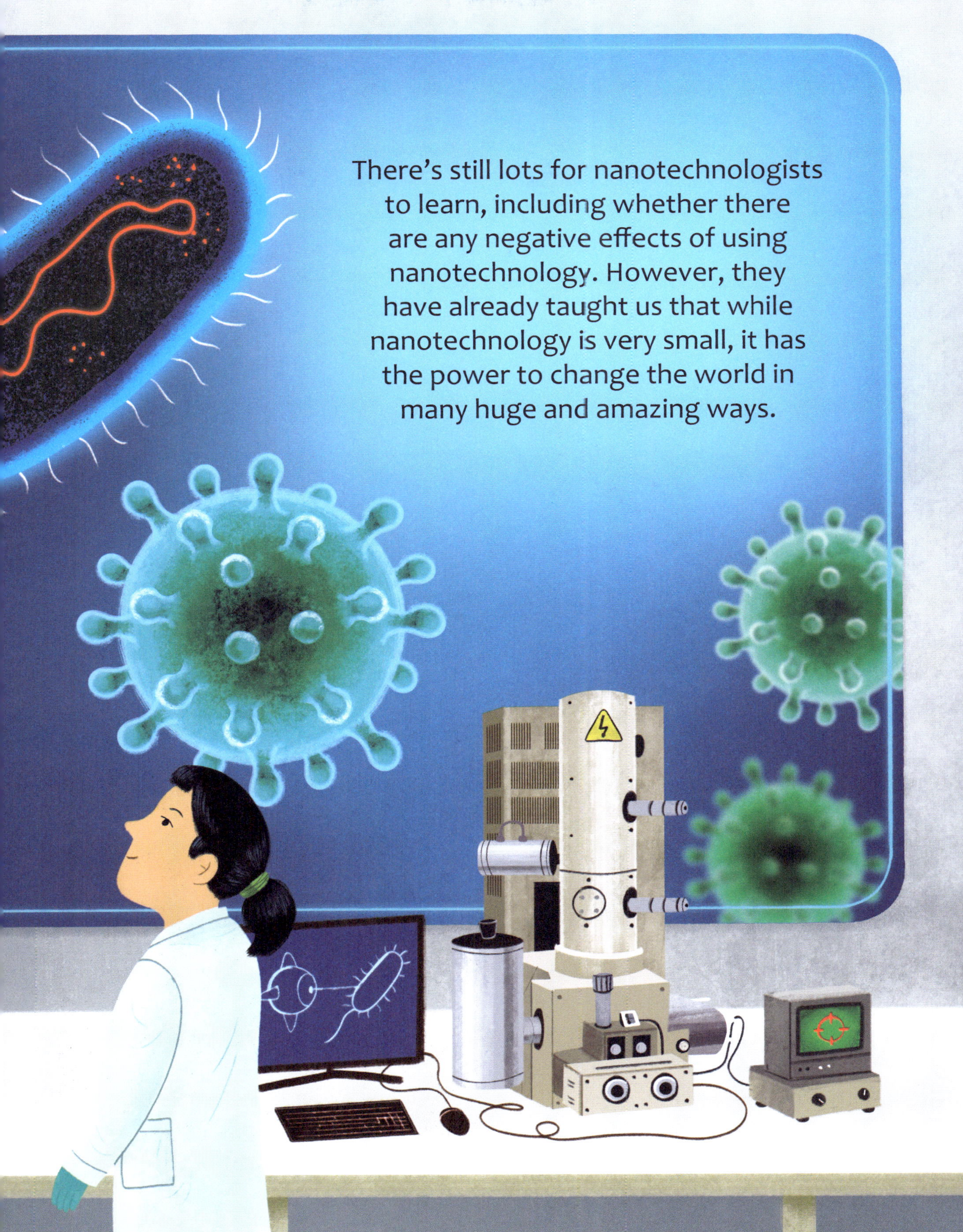

There's still lots for nanotechnologists to learn, including whether there are any negative effects of using nanotechnology. However, they have already taught us that while nanotechnology is very small, it has the power to change the world in many huge and amazing ways.

*Hidden*

# NANOTECHNOLOGY

**Humans have been using, or observing the impact of, nanomaterials for centuries without knowing it. Here are some mind-blowing examples...**

## DAMASCUS STEEL

This **hand-forged** metal has been made into swords for hundreds of years. With an iconic wave pattern, it's known for being very sharp and strong. In 2006, microscopes revealed the steel's secret is carbon nanotubes!

## STAINED GLASS

**Medieval** stained-glass artists added gold and silver to their glass. Nanoparticles of these metals helped create bright and long-lasting glass artwork. Gold made bright red glass, while silver made bright yellow.

## DICHROIC GLASS

Glass can be crafted to change under different lights or angles! This method dates back at least 1,700 years. While ancient glassmakers didn't know about nanoparticles, glass changing from clear to green, red, or yellow is due to nanoparticles!

## ANCIENT CONCRETE

Concrete used in Roman structures like the Pantheon is amazingly strong. It can even heal itself when exposed to seawater! Modern scientists have discovered it's the concrete's nanostructure that makes it so tough.

## PEACOCK FEATHERS

Peacock feathers are an example of natural nanotechnology! Their bright blues, greens, and yellows are so bold because of the nanostructure of the feathers, which causes light to reflect in beautiful ways.

*Amazing*

# NANOTECHNOLOGY FACTS

**There's so much to discover about the world of nanotechnology. Do you know the answers to some big questions about the world of tiny things?**

## HOW DO NANOTECHNOLOGISTS SEE NANOTECHNOLOGY?

With incredibly strong microscopes! Scanning probe microscopes are just one of the tools that scientists use to see and control nanoparticles and nanomachines.

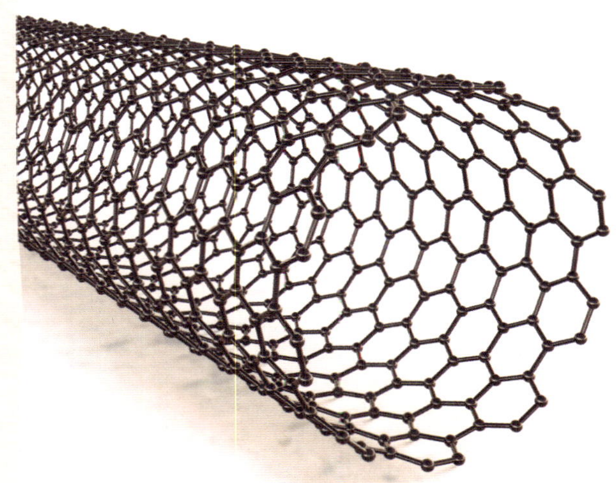

## HOW DIFFERENT ARE MATERIALS ON THE NANOSCALE?

Very! For example, while the natural form of carbon – graphite – is normally soft, scientists have discovered that packing it into a nanotube makes it very hard!

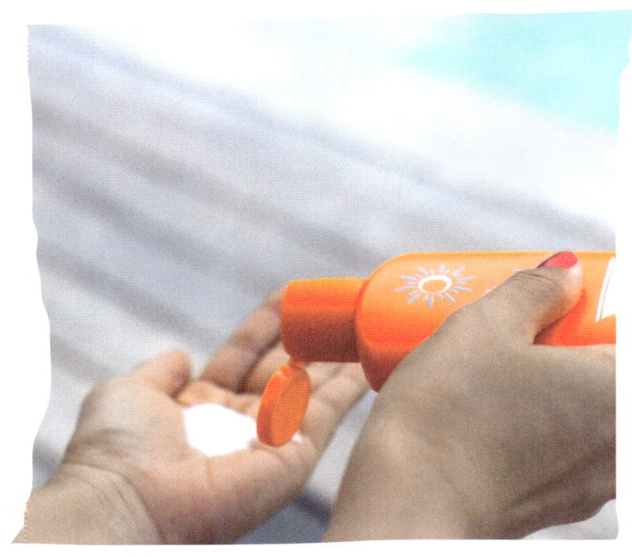

## IS NANOTECHNOLOGY ALWAYS A SOLID OBJECT?

No! Nanoparticles are often used in liquids to improve them. In sunscreens, they help the liquid spread more easily and give the body better protection from the Sun's harmful rays.

## HOW CAN NANOTECHNOLOGY HELP THE NATURAL WORLD?

Scientists have created sponges that could change the way we clean up oil spills. The sponges can collect more than 30 times their weight in oil and do so without harming plants or animals.

## WHAT IS THE WORLD'S SMALLEST CREATION?

There are lots of amazing records, but one of the most impressive is the world's smallest 3D map. Created in 2012, this map of the world is so small you could fit 1,000 of them on a single grain of salt!

# GLOSSARY

**Absorb** – to soak up.

**Acid rain** – harmful rain that can damage things over time.

**Atmosphere** – the gases that surround a planet.

**Atoms** – the smallest building blocks of matter that make up everything around us.

**Bacteria** – tiny living things that can be found in all natural environments.

**Bloodstream** – the path blood takes through the body.

**Body tissue** – a group of cells that perform a specific task inside the body, like muscles.

**Cells** – the smallest parts of a living thing.

**Chemicals** – substances made up of the same tiny building blocks. They are often made by humans.

**Clean energy** – energy that does not harm the planet.

**Climate change** – a change in the weather over a long time.

**Diseases** – medical conditions that cause part of a living thing to no longer work properly.

**Gases** – tiny, usually invisible, particles in the air.

**Hand-forged** – a metal item that's shaped by hand.

**Medieval** – a period of time in Europe that lasted from around 500 to 1500 CE, sometimes called the Middle Ages.

**Modifying** – changing something for a specific reason.

**Nanobots** – robots that are measured on the nanoscale (see below).

**Nanoparticles** – particles that are measured on the nanoscale (see below).

**Nanoscale** – something that's so small it's measured in nanometers/nanometres.

**Nutrients** – substances or ingredients that plants and animals need to live and grow.

**Organisms** – living things. They range in size from tiny bacteria to huge whales.

**Organs** – parts of the body (made of tissue) that do special jobs. The heart is an organ.

**Ozone layer** – a layer of gas high in the sky that shields Earth from the Sun's UV rays (see below).

**Pollution** – harmful materials that have been released into the environment.

**Radiation** – a type of energy that can harm living things if it's strong or in large amounts.

**Robots** – machines that can move and do tasks by themselves.

**UV rays** – invisible energy from the Sun that can help or harm, depending on its strength.

# HOW DO I SAY?

**Dichroic**
dye-CROW-ick

**Nanotechnologists**
nah-noh-TECK-noh-luh-jists

**Nanotechnology**
nah-noh-TECK-noh-luh-jee

# THE BIG QUESTIONS ANSWERED

**This is more than just a series of books; it is a complete resource. Accompanying each book is a variety of FREE material to engage curious kids with science.**

**www.thebigquestionsanswered.com**

Use the QR code to visit the website, download free resources, and discover other books in the series.

On the website, find out incredible things about nanotechnologists, including what they do, some of their greatest discoveries, and the people who have made a difference in this field of science.

**The material is also available for home or classroom use, supporting all the information in this book.**

**Teachers' & Parents' Resources**

With discussion prompts, questions, and extra information around key topics.

**Activity Pack**

Fun activities including creative writing, word searches, and more.

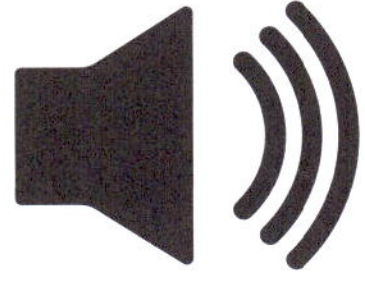

**Audio Book**

Experience this book in audio, narrated by a professional voice actor.

**The Big Questions Answered is published by Beetle Books. Beetle Books is an imprint of Hungry Tomato Ltd.**

First published in 2025 by Hungry Tomato Ltd
F15, Old Bakery Studios, Blewetts Wharf, Malpas Road,
Truro, Cornwall, TR1 1QH, UK.

ISBN 9781835691489



**Copyright © 2025 Hungry Tomato Ltd**

No part of this publication may be reproduced, stored in a retrieval system, or transmitted in any form or by any means, electronic, mechanical, photocopying, recording, or otherwise, without prior written permission of the copyright owner.



A CIP catalog record for this book is available from the British Library.

With thanks to:
Editors: Holly Thornton and Jenny Rowan
Designers: Meg Holbrook and Amy Harvey
Consultant: Professor Gino Hrkac
The team at Beehive Illustration

Information in this book is up to date as of the time of writing.

Printed and bound in China.

Picture Credits:
(t = top, b = bottom, m = middle, l = left, r = right)
Shutterstock: Artsiom P 35mr; CGS Graphics 35tl; oleJohny 34bl; satoriphoto 33ml; Thorsteinn Asgeirsson 33br; Tunatura 32mr; RethaAretha 34mr; Wirestock Creators 35bl.